unBEElievables

honeybee poems and paintings
by Douglas Florian

BEACH LANE BOOKS • New York London Toronto Sydney New Delhi

BEACH LANE BOOKS

An imprint of Simon & Schuster Children's
Publishing Division • 1230 Avenue of the Americas,
New York, New York 10020 • Copyright © 2012 by Douglas
Florian • All rights reserved, including the right of reproduction
in whole or in part in any form. • BEACH LANE BOOKS is a trademark of
Simon & Schuster, Inc. • For information about special discounts for bulk
purchases, please contact Simon & Schuster Special Sales at 1-866-506-1949
or business@simonandschuster.com. • The Simon & Schuster Speakers Bureau
can bring authors to your live event. For more information or to book an event,
contact the Simon & Schuster Speakers Bureau at 1-866-248-3049 or visit our website
at www.simonspeakers.com. • Book design by Lauren Rille • The text for this book is set in
Neutra. • The illustrations for this book were created with gouache paint, colored pencils,
and collage on primed paper bags. • Manufactured in China • 1217 SCP •
• 6   8   10   9   7   5   •
Library of Congress Cataloging-in-Publication Data • Florian, Douglas.
• UnBEElievables: honeybee poems and paintings / Douglas Florian.
—1st ed. • p. cm. • ISBN 978-1-4424-2652-8 (hardcover) • 1. Bees—
Juvenile poetry. 2. Honeybee—Juvenile poetry. 3. Bees—
Ecology—Juvenile poetry. 4. Children's poetry, American.
I. Title. II. Title: Unbelievables. • PS3556.L589U63 2012
• 811'.54—dc22 • 2011005613 • ISBN 978-1-4424-4676-2
(eBook)

For my mother, Edith,
of blessed memory,
a sweet soul and a lover of literature

Welcome!

Welcome, welcome to our hive!

Honeycomb home where we thrive!

Into light and sweetness dive!

Guards greet you when you arrive!

For hive harmony we strive!

We keep busy stayin' alive!

Welcome, welcome to our hive!

Honeycomb home where we thrive.

Honeybees will often use a hollow tree trunk as a site to build a hive. They may live there for several years. The structure of the hive is called a honeycomb, and it is made of many hexagonal (six-sided) cells of beeswax.

Bee Anatomy

Lovely legs,
Lovely hue.
Lovely long
Antennae, too.
Lovely eyes,
Lovely wings.
But ouch!
How in the **end**
It stings!

A honeybee's body has three segments: a head, a thorax, and an abdomen. The head has two antennae that are used for touch, taste, and even smell. Below the antennae are two large compound eyes with thousands of tiny lenses that detect motion and three small simple eyes that are sensitive to light. The thorax has three pairs of legs and two pairs of wings. The abdomen has the digestive and reproductive organs and, in female bees only, a stinger at the tip.

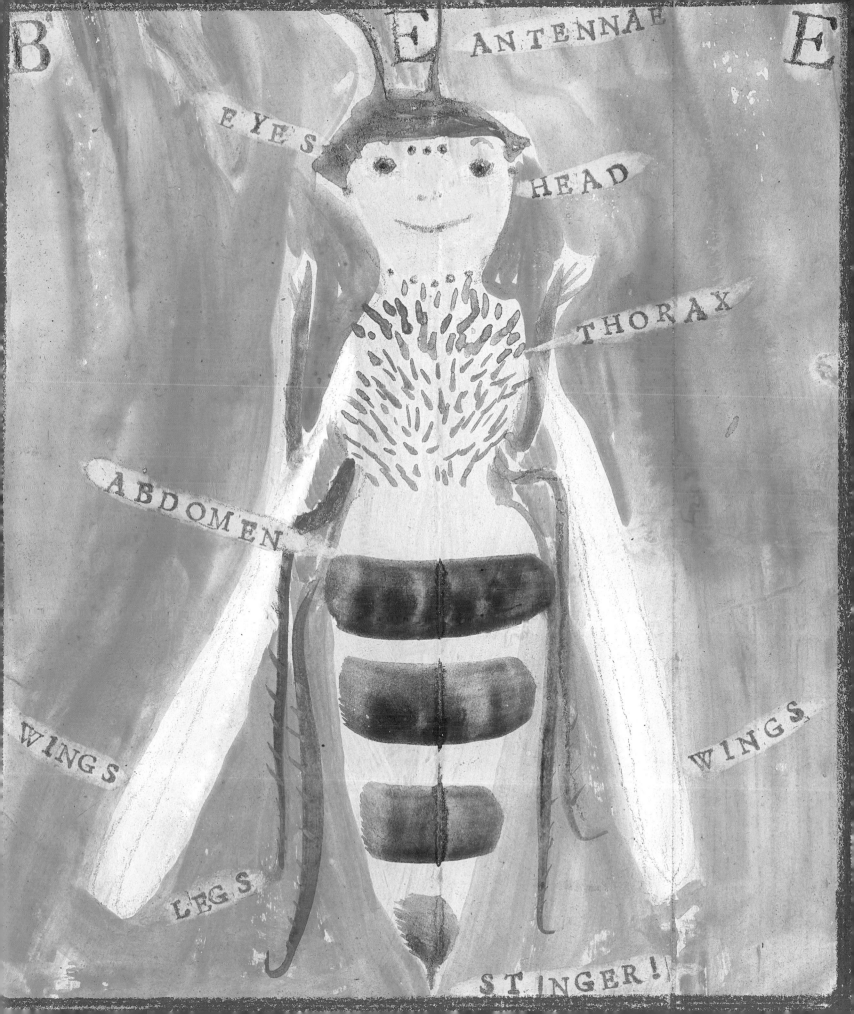

Queen Bee

I am no ordinary bee:
I'm royalty, a queen, you see!
I don't just raise a family—
I rule a whole society!
Each day I lay two thousand eggs.
Believe me—that's tough on the legs!
My doting daughters feed my belly,
And **I** was raised on royal jelly.
My princely sons are known as drones—
Not **one** of those boys ever phones!
When it's too crammed,
Then I take wing.
With such a life—
Who needs a king?!

The queen bee is fed royal jelly, a protein-rich paste, and eventually becomes the largest bee in the hive. Worker bees tend to all her needs, feeding and grooming her around the clock. During breeding season, the queen lays as many as 2,000 eggs a day, creating a colony of up to 80,000 bees.

Drone

BROTHER!

Yo, BROTHER!

Bee-have in your hive!

Hey, DRONE!

Don't MOAN!

Don't GROAN!

And don't JIVE!

Your fate is to mate!

Don't be late!

Find a queen!

Hey, BIG EYES!

Hey, BUG EYES!

Be COOL!

Make the scene!

All drone bees in a hive are brothers. Their only job is to mate with a queen bee from another hive, and they have very large eyes to help them find one. Drones are stingless and cannot defend the hive or forage for food. After mating, they die.

Worker Bees

Sister.
    Sister.
Sister.
    Sister.
Not one brother.
Not one mister.
See us sisters work all day,
Dawn to dusk—no time to play.
We must feed the needy queen,
Drones, and babies—
And we clean!
When it's hot, we fan the air.
Have the hive in good repair.
Always working,
    building,
  slaving.
Never
Ever
Miss-bee-having.

All worker bees in a hive are sisters. Their most important job is to feed the queen, the drones, and the larvae. They must also make beeswax and build the honeycomb, clean the hive, guard the hive's entrance, fan the hive to keep it cool, collect nectar from flowers to make honey, and carry pollen from flower to flower.

Summer Hummer

I'm the hummer of summer,

So busy with buzz.

A never-humdrummer

All covered with fuzz.

I'm a nectar collector.

Make wax to the max.

A beehive protector.

I never relax.

I'm a lover of clover.

A seeker of scent.

A zigzag flyover—

A thing heaven-sent.

I'm a dancer, a prancer.

My own pollen nation.

A flower enhancer.

A summer sensation.

Like all insects, honeybees are cold-blooded and most active
during the summer months. In winter they cluster together
for warmth, feeding on stored honey. There are as many as
20,000 known species of bees, but fewer than ten known
species of honeybees.

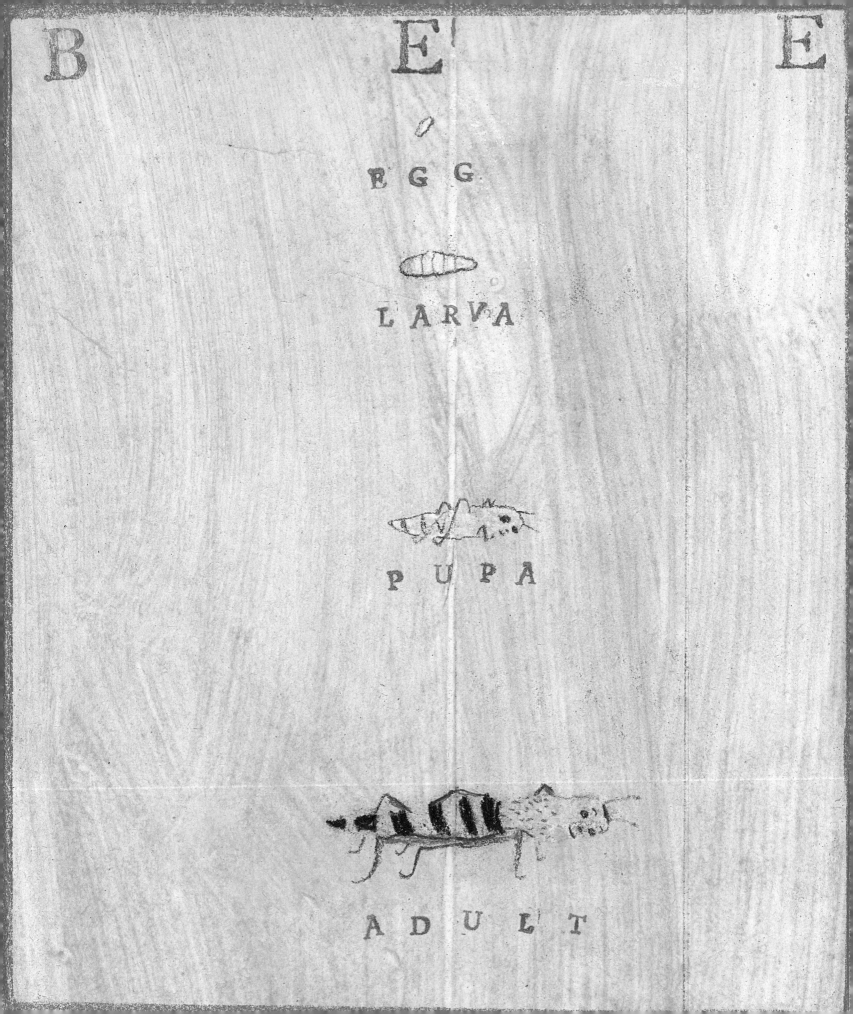

Bee-coming

From egg I hatch in just three days,
Bee-ginning my new larval phase.
I dwell in a six-sided cell.
My cozy home bee-fits me well.
Then as a pupa, how I change,
Bee-coming something else, so strange!
My body slowly grows until
I'm truly un-bee-lievable!

The bee life cycle begins when the queen bee lays an egg in a
honeycomb cell. After the larva hatches, worker bees feed it royal
jelly and then beebread, a mixture of honey and pollen. (A queen
bee larva skips the beebread and gets royal jelly continuously.)
The cell is then sealed with beeswax by a worker. Inside the cell,
the larva spins a cocoon and changes into a pupa, growing legs,
wings, and other organs, until it breaks free from the cell as an
adult bee.

Waggle Dance

We dance. We prance.
    We waggle. We wiggle.
Come glance at our stance
    While we jiggle and wriggle.
Our dance round and round
    Shows where flowers are found.
And our figure eights
    Show where pollen awaits.

Scout bees are workers who perform different dances to alert the other bees as to where flowers may be found. If flowers are nearby, they perform a simple "round dance," moving in loops in alternating directions. But if flowers are farther away, they perform a more intricate "waggle dance," a figure-eight pattern.

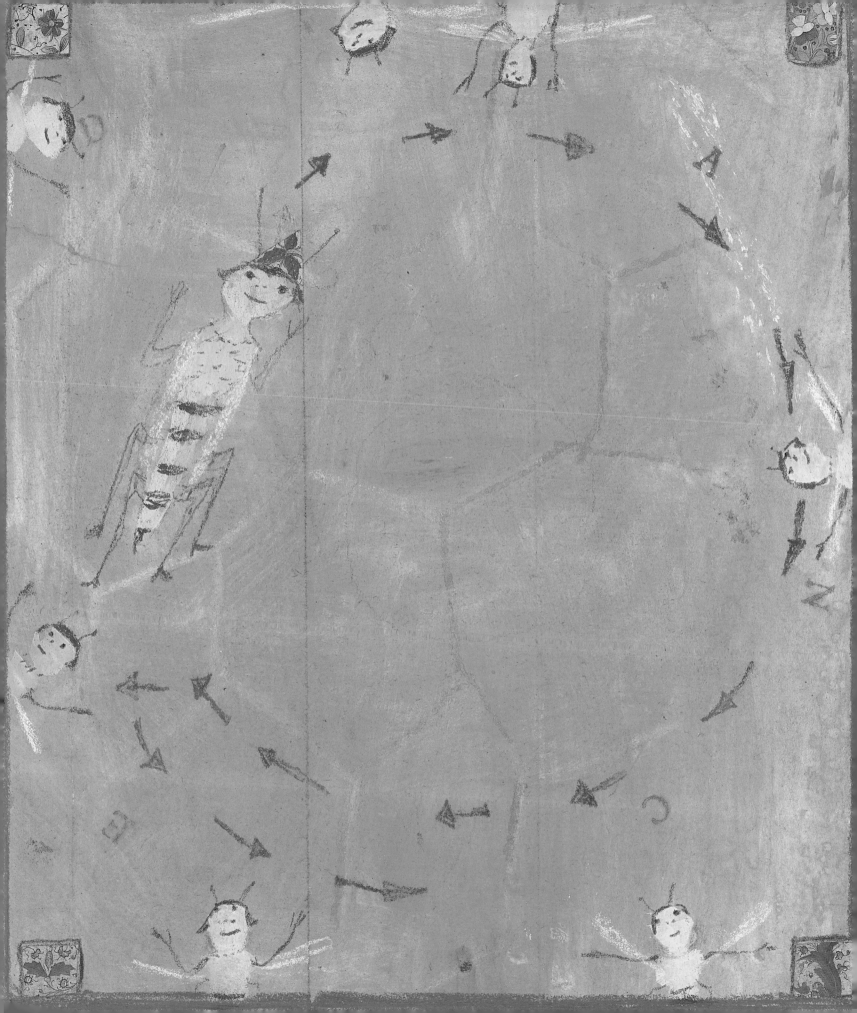

Honey

So many blossoms!
So many flowers!
So much flying—
Hours and hours!
So much nectar
Needed to eat
So **honey**
All will end up sweet!

Bees begin to make honey by taking nectar from flowers and depositing droplets of it inside the hive's honey cells. Then they fan the nectar with their wings to remove moisture. Later they cap the cells with wax, which helps the nectar thicken into honey. A colony of bees may visit more than a million flowers to make just one pound of honey.

Pollen

Pollen on my legs and feet.

Pollen on my wings that beat.

Pollen on my cheeks and chin.

Pollen on my abdomen.

I just took a pollen shower.

I'm a fuzzy, flying flower!

One of bees' most important roles in nature is a process called pollination. When a bee lands on a flower to collect nectar, the flower's powdery pollen sticks to her antennae, her fuzz, and her legs. When she moves to the next flower, she deposits some of the pollen, enabling the plant to reproduce.

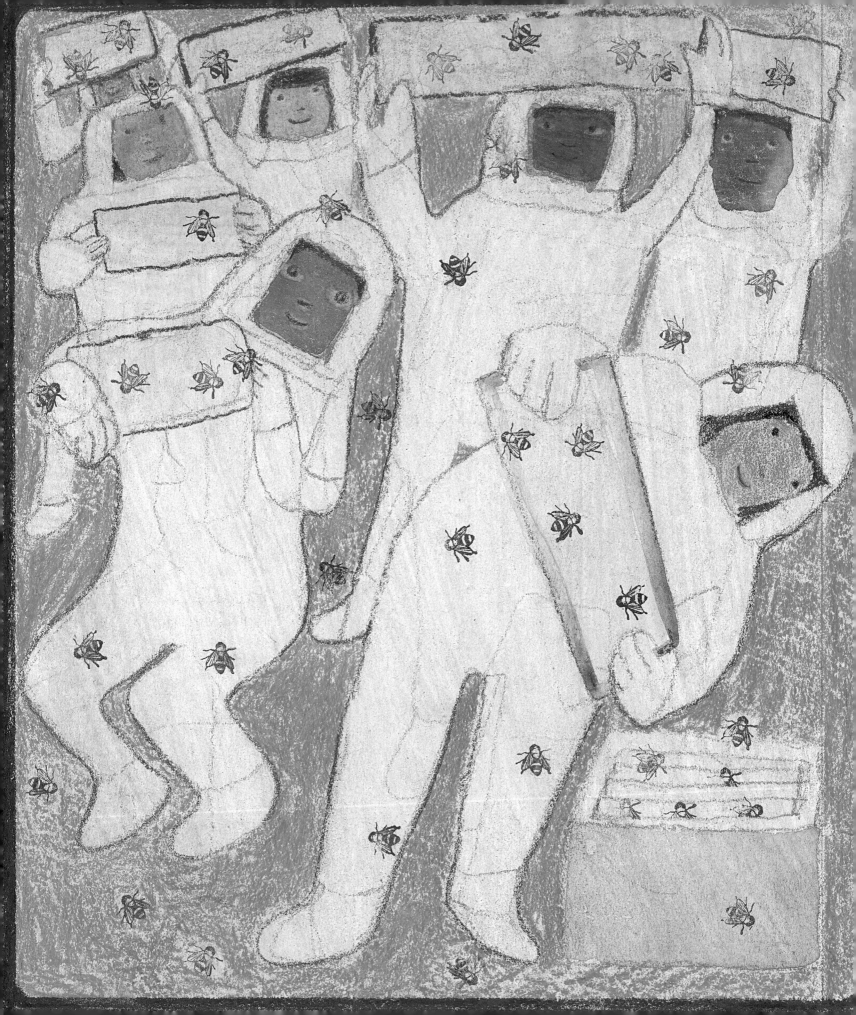

The Beekeepers

We're the boys-in-the-hood.
(Girls-in-the-hood too.)
We always wear white—
The beekeeping crew.
Check out our white gloves.
Check out our white boots.
Hey, dig our white veils
And baggy white suits.
We're keeping the bees.
We fret and we fuss.
We're keeping the bees.
Or do they keep us?

Beekeepers have been harvesting honey from man-made hives for more than 4,000 years. In the past beekeepers used woven straw baskets called skeps as hives, but today most use wooden or plastic boxes. Beekeepers wear gloves, boots, and hooded suits (usually white) to protect them from bee stings. They also may use a bee smoker to generate bee-calming smoke.

Bees Buzz

All day we bees
Just buzz and buzz.
That's what we duzz
And duzz and duzz.
Why are we full
Of fuzz and fuzz?
Bee-cuzz bee-cuzz
The fuzz the fuzz
Helps pollen stick
To uzz to uzz.

Bees beat their wings rapidly when they fly. This causes the air around them to vibrate, and the vibration creates bees' signature buzzing sound. The fuzzy hairs on bees' bodies have an electrostatic charge, which helps attract a flower's pollen grains.

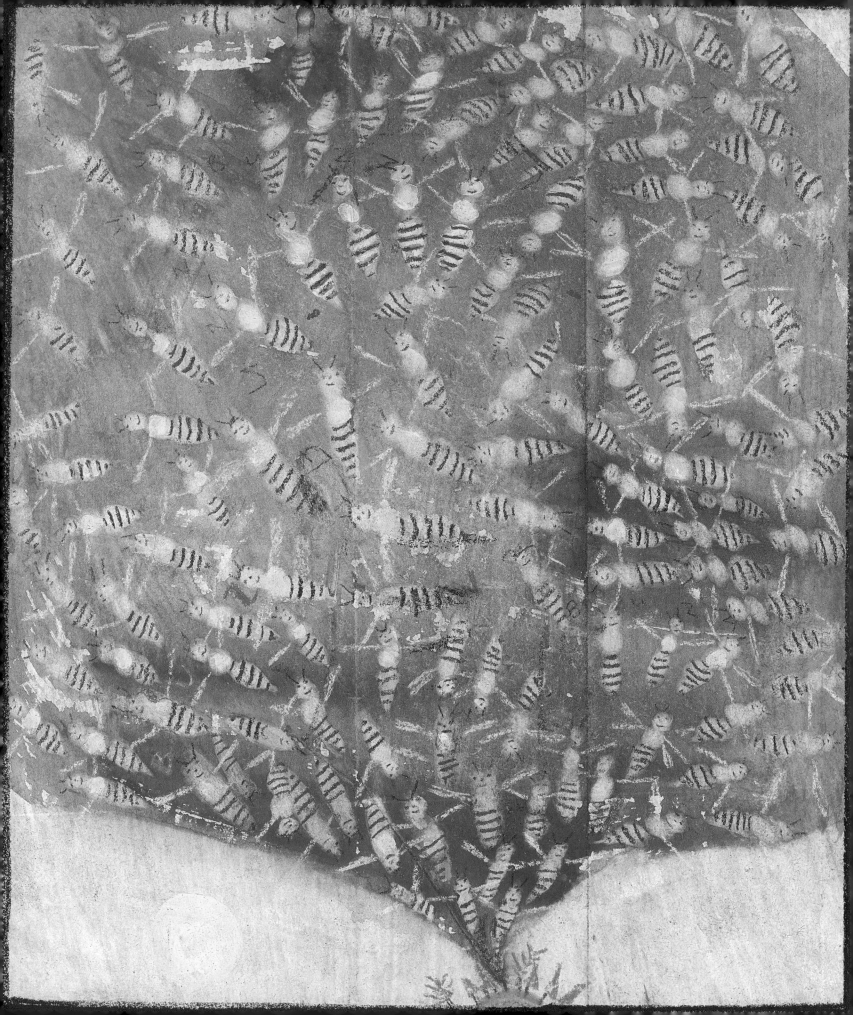

Swarm

When it's too crowded, then we form
A cloud of bees that's called a swarm.
We crowd and cram, we pull and push
Upon a post or branch or bush.
Each scout seeks out a nice new nest.
We pick the site that suits us best.
And then we build a honeycomb—
A busy, buzzy, home **sweet** home.

When the hive gets to be too crowded, the queen sets out with a swarm of loyal workers to start a new colony. Scout bees search for a new nest site while the other bees wait, crowding together on a branch, post, or bush. After the best site is selected, the worker bees secrete wax and then begin building a new honeycomb.

Where Are the Bees?

Bees give us sweet honey.

They pollinate flowers.

The beeswax in candles

Keeps burning for hours.

But some hives have vanished,

Some bees disappeared.

(From mites or pollution

Or illness, it's feared.)

Let's hope that before long

The bees come back strong,

And hives will be humming,

Bees buzzing along.

Since 2006 thousands of honeybee colonies have disappeared. Scientists believe mites, viruses, pesticides, or fungi may be responsible for what is called Colony Collapse Disorder. It is important that we try to remedy this situation, not only for the sake of bees and their honey, but also because many crops and wild plants depend on bees for pollination.

BEEbliography

Benjamin, Alison, and Brian McCallum. *Keeping Bees and Making Honey*. Cincinnati: David & Charles, 2008.

Ellis, Hattie. *Sweetness and Light: The Mysterious History of the Honeybee*. New York: Three Rivers Press, 2004.

Micucci, Charles. *The Life and Times of the Honeybee*. New York: Houghton Mifflin, 1995.

Savage, Candace. *Bees: Nature's Little Wonders*. Vancouver: Greystone Books, 2008.

Further Reading

The Bee Database Project: http://research.amnh.org/iz/bee-database-project

Articles about bees from the *New York Times*: http://topics.nytimes.com/top/news/science/topics/bees/index.html